Make Your Own Sourdough Starter

Capture and Harness the Wild Yeast

Written by Teresa L Greenway of Northwest Sourdough
Updated and revised version June 9 2017

For online Sourdough Baking Courses visit:
http://www.northwestsourdough.com

For a day by day video tutorial on how to make a sourdough starter check on Youtube at Northwest Sourdough's channel.

To read my memoir see, "Reach for Joy" by Tessy Reys (my pseudonym) on Amazon.

Contents

Introduction

Bakers have used wild fermentation for centuries to leaven their bread. Fermentation is a natural process which doesn't need much help to get going. It was once thought that the wild yeast was "caught" from the air or the surroundings. Although that is possible, it isn't what usually happens. Grains are coated with microorganisms suitable for fermenting. The same process is at work when grapes are pressed to make wine. Grapes are covered with the microorganisms suitable for making wine. So the grains and the grapes bring their own fermentation buddies with them.

Basically, you just mix flour and water, give it some time and you will end up with a sourdough starter that you can use to make great sourdough bread with. Some bakers make fresh sourdough starter or "levain" on a regular basis. Others swear by grandma's century old starter brought over with the covered wagons.

Microbiologically, once a starter is stable and kept healthy it doesn't actually get any better with age. But a little romance with the story of the family starter grandma kept alive on the wagon train is perfectly fine. As long as the starter works, produces great flavorful bread and is healthy, it doesn't really matter much. This book is an introduction to sourdough bread baking. It will help you learn to make your own sourdough starter and motherdough pre-ferment.

So let's get right down to it and make some sourdough starter. I will be giving you several types of starters you can make including a " motherdough" pre-ferment. You can also follow videos on how to make sourdough starter and bake sourdough bread on my You Tube channel: Northwest Sourdough

How to Make Your Own Sourdough Starter

How to Make and Care for Your Sourdough Starter

When you add water to some flour, a fascinating process is set in motion. The microorganisms that live on the grain, which has been ground into flour, begin to digest the starches and proteins in the flour, producing, sugar, gas and enzymatic activity.

This process is called fermentation. Fermentation renders flour more digestible by breaking down phytates present in the grain and predigesting the gluten and starch. During fermentation, starches are broken down into sugars for the yeasts to feed resulting in the production of gasses. Strands of gluten (called Glutenin and Gliadin), present in some grains, particularly in wheat, bond together, forming a sticky web which traps gas bubbles and causes dough to rise..

To start this process, it is helpful to have a culture of these microorganisms. In everyday language, one of these cultures is called a sourdough starter. If you can't obtain a sourdough starter from someone, you can make your own. Making your own sourdough starter is easy and fun, it just takes a few ingredients and time (about two weeks). When you are finished, you will be ready to bake sourdough bread in your own kitchen.

Gather Your Equipment and Ingredients

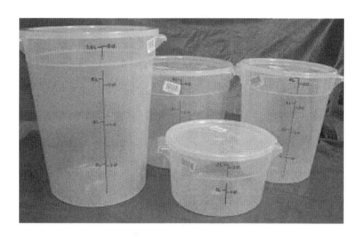

The Container

For the container which you will use to keep your sourdough starter in, use a food grade plastic container (a large yogurt container or plastic ware will do fine), a crock pot or a bowl with a lid which can hold around 32- 48 fluid ounces (around 2 quarts or 2 liters), something that will hold around 4 - 8 cups. Do not use a container that is made of reactive metal. Also, do not use a reactive metal implement to stir your starter with. Stainless steel is fine to use. You can use a glass container, but there is a risk of getting pieces of glass in your starter if you accidentally hit the edge with something.

A lid for the container is important because the starter should be covered to keep out dust and insects, especially pesky fruit flies. It will also slow down the rate at which the starter evaporates. You can have a snug fitting or a loose lid, either one works as the oxygen is good to help get the fermentation going (for some of the yeast activity) but most the micro-organisms themselves are anaerobic (especially the Lactic Acid Bacteria) and don't require oxygen.

Flour
Use fresh flour. Unbleached white flour, whole wheat or other whole grain flour can be used. If the flour is old or has been stored in a damp place, it can be moldy, have flour bugs, or have a rancid or undesirable taste. The microorganisms necessary to get your starter fermenting are abundant in fresh flour, especially rye and whole grain flour. Bleached/bromated flour is not especially useful for making a starter; the chemicals can interfere with the process. A blend of regular (all purpose) flour and a whole grain like wheat or rye is a good way to start. Make a mixture of (50/50) white flour and some whole grain flour and store it in a container to feed your starter with.

Water
Use pure water. Try to use water that doesn't contain chlorine or other chemicals in it, if possible. The microorganisms that make up the starter are sensitive to chemicals. If you only have access to tap water, set the tap water out in a container overnight to allow the chlorine to escape. Lightly cover the container with a cloth to keep out dust. You can use filtered water for making a starter. If you have to use bottled water, try to obtain water that has not

been distilled, the minerals in the water help keep the starter healthy.

Juice

Juice can be used in a mixture of half juice and half water for the first four days to jumpstart your new sourdough starter. Pineapple, orange or other types of juice add acidity to the starter and help encourage the correct microorganisms to thrive. It isn't necessary but it can help speed up the process. Read about "The Pineapple Juice Solution" by Debra Wink

Salt

Salt is mentioned here because it can be used in small amounts to control over-fermenting. It warmer climates and with some types of flour, a sourdough starter can have trouble fermenting too fast. Salt helps control fermentation by inhibiting the enzymatic action (especially Protease). Use sea salt or salt that has no chemical additives if you can. There are many wonderful sea salts available on the market now. A good sea salt adds not only flavor but minerals to your baking products.

The process

When you mix together flour and water, several things happen. The flour becomes hydrated, the gluten strands begin to bond, microorganisms already present in the flour proliferate and enzymes break down starches into sugars to feed the microorganisms. The microorganisms are mainly yeasts and bacteria. There can be many types of bacteria present in the flour but the one you want to encourage are the bacteria that thrive in acidic conditions (lactic acid bacteria). During the first four days after you make the flour and water mixture, the bacteria fight for dominance. After four days, the starter will naturally become more acidic and the correct bacteria establish themselves in their new home. That is why during the first four days, when the microorganisms are fighting for dominance, the starter can smell terrible, like dirty socks or even vomit (yea, really gross). At this point a lot of bakers will toss the starter because they think it went bad. But actually it's just a stage on the journey. By day five or six the starter begins to smell more fruity and yeasty, like you expect it to. So don't give up, keep feeding your starter and be patient. This is also the reason why using half water/half juice can help jumpstart the process. It helps the correct microorganisms establish themselves more quickly.

Sometimes during the process you might notice that your sourdough starter smells like acetone or very sharp. If that happens, it means you are not feeding it enough and you either need to feed the starter more food during feeding time, feed it more often, or both.

How to Make a 100% Hydration Starter

Start small, and then increase amounts when you are ready to bake.

Day 1: In your container mix together:

- **30 grams of white flour**
- **30 grams of whole grain flour (whole wheat, rye, spelt etc)**
- **60 grams of water** (or juice, see note below)

Keep the container at room temperature between 68-78F. Cover the container with a snug fitting lid (it doesn't need to breath but oxygen helps jumpstart the process).

Day 2: Stir the mixture well. Don't feed. You don't want to dilute the organisms with food until you actually see fermentation. You have 120 grams of starter.

Day 3: If the mixture has good fermentation activity, discard about half of the starter and feed the starter with a mixture of 40 grams of water (or juice) and 40 grams of flour (20 grams of white and 20 grams of whole grain or a mixture of the two as long as the total is 40 grams). Stir well and cover. If the mixture has no or very little activity, don't feed it, just stir and allow it to set another day. You'll have around 140 grams of starter.

Day 4: Discard all but 30 grams of starter and feed with 50 grams of water and 50 grams of the flour mixture, stirring well. You'll have 130 grams of starter. This is a nice amount of starter to maintain the starter. You would feed it more once it's stable and you want to bake with it. At this point you should begin to feed your starter twice a day. The amount of starter is small and so is the food, you can feed it once a day, but it will be much more vigorous and healthy if you feed it every 12 hours. Do not keep the starter in the refrigerator at this point unless you have to because of excessive heat.

Day 5: Continue to discard all except about 30 grams of starter and continue to feed with:
- **50 grams flour (any type you choose)**
- **50 grams water (juice is no longer necessary if you were using it).**

Juice is only used for the first four days to help the acid loving bacteria thrive. You want to encourage the lactic acid bacteria and you do that by using a bit of acidic juice. It isn't necessary but it can help. By day 6 or 7 if your starter is active and fermenting at a good rate, you could increase the amount of food (flour and water) in the evening and make up some pancakes, waffles, etc. by the next morning. If you need 200 grams of starter for pancakes, then just discard all but 30-50 grams of starter and feed your starter 100 grams of flour and 100 grams of water. That way you have the 200 grams of starter and 30 -50 grams left over to feed again to continue your starter.

Day 6 – 14:
Continue to discard all but 30 – 50 grams of starter and feed 50- 60 grams of water and 50-60 grams of flour each day. Do not refrigerate it at this point. Keep your new starter at room temperature. The amounts of starter and food are just a suggestion. You basically need to have less starter and more food so the microorganisms will have plenty to feed on. If you don't discard, there will be too many microorganism and not enough food then they will begin to starve and get sick. The amount of starter isn't critical for keeping the 100% hydration the food it. Just remember to always feed the same weight of flour and water and your starter will always be at 100% hydration.

**See "The Pineapple Solution," by Debra Wink for an explanation of why pineapple juice can be used to jumpstart a new sourdough starter (do a Google search).*

If your starter seems sluggish or just won't ferment well, discard more of the starter and feed a **higher ratio** of flour and water. For instance discard all but a small amount of starter (30 grams) and then feed it 80 grams of water and 80 grams of flour (or even 100 grams of each). See if the higher ratio of food jump starts it.

When room temperatures are warm, the starter will need to have a higher ratio of food to stay healthy and need to be fed more often. Heat speed up the rate of fermentation, more fermentation activity means you need to feed and care for your starter more often.

After day 14, your starter should be able to double in 4-8 hours and it will be stable enough to keep in the refrigerator in between use. See more about testing your starter later in this book.

How to Make a 166% Hydration Starter
(Used in my book, "Discovering Sourdough.")

It might not look bubbly, but it's got great leavening power!
To make a 166% hydration starter, you would add together
flour and salt based on volume, for instance 1/2 cup of water
and 1/2 cup of flour. I used this hydration in my book
because it is easy for newbies to work with, especially if they
want to get a starter going while their new kitchen scale is
coming in the mail.

You would follow the same steps as the 100% starter, only use the same volume measurements instead of the same weight measurements.

If you have a scale and want to measure for a 166% starter, it has 166 grams of water to every 100 grams of flour. So you could mix half those amounts to get begin with- 83 grams of water and 50 grams of flour.

It might look like this:

Day 1: In your container mix together:
- **1/4 cup of white flour (or 34 grams)**
- **1/4 cup of whole grain flour (34 grams [whole wheat, rye, spelt etc])**
- **1/2 cup of water** (or juice, see note below) (113 grams)

Keep the container at room temperature between 68-78F. Cover the container with a cloth or a loose fitting cover.

Day 2: Stir the mixture well. Don't feed.

Day 3: If the mixture has good fermentation activity, discard half and feed the starter with the same amounts shown above on day 1. Stir well and cover. If the mixture has no or very little activity, just stir and allow it to set another day.

Day 4: Repeat day 3.

Day 5: Discard all but about 1/3 cup of the starter and feed it with: (we'll use smaller amounts until you need to use it for baking).
- **1/3 cup flour (any type you choose [45 grams])**

- **1/3 cup water (juice is no longer necessary if you were using it [75 grams water]).**

By day 6 or 7 if your starter is active and fermenting at a good rate, you could add a lot more of the feed (flour and water) in the evening and make up some pancakes, waffles, etc. by the next morning.

Day 6 – 14:

Continue to discard about 2/3 rds of your starter and feed it the same amount (by volume) of flour and water each day. Do not refrigerate it at this point. Keep your new starter at room temperature.

A thinner starter ferments more quickly but is easier to incorporate into a dough mixture.

**See "The Pineapple Solution," by Debra Wink for an explanation of why pineapple juice can be used to jumpstart a new sourdough starter (do a Google search).

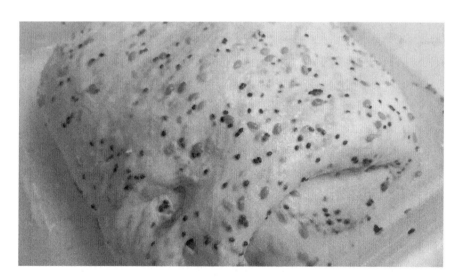

How to Change the Hydration Level

It's actually quite easy to change hydration levels for your starter. Discard most of the starter and then begin to feed it the hydration level you wish to have. If you have a 100% hydration starter and wish to have a 166% hydration starter, just pour out most of your 100% starter and begin to feed your starter with the amounts that make up a 166% starter ie: (166grams of water to every 100 grams of flour or 83 grams of water and 50 grams of flour).

If you have a 166% hydration starter and wish to change it to a 100% hydration starter, pour out most of the starter and begin to feed it equal weights of flour and water ie: (100 grams of water to every 100 grams of flour).

The same is true if you wish to have a 60% motherdough. Take a portion of your 100% starter and begin feeding it (60 grams of water to every 100 grams of flour). If you wish to be more exact you would need a hydration calculator (there are several free ones available online). I have included a formula for a 60% motherdough in this book. See the chapter "How to Make a Motherdough at 60% Hydration."

Convert a 100% Starter to a 166% Starter

This is how to change a 100% hydration starter into a 166% starter (for use in formulas where it calls for 166% hydration but you have a 100% hydration starter).
Most of the formulas in my books, "Discovering Sourdough," are based off of one cup of 166% sourdough starter which equals 9 ounces/254 grams of starter (at 166%).

Convert your 100% hydration starter to 166% easily by:

Combine 191 grams of starter at 100% hydration and 63 grams of water, you will have approximately 1 cup/ 9oz of starter at 166%.

191 grams (100% starter) plus 63 grams of water = I cup/ 9ounces/254 grams (of starter at 166% hydration)

When Can I Use My Starter?

After the first week if you want to try using your starter, begin by trying some sourdough pancakes, biscuits or scones. Make sure to feed your starter extra so you have enough for your sourdough recipe. During the second week you can try to bake a loaf of bread and see how well it does.

Doubling Test

One way to tell if a starter is ready to bake bread is to put some freshly fed starter in a clear or translucent container, mark the level, and then see if the starter doubles over the next 4 to 6 hours.

Testing Your Starter's Capability

Years ago I set up an experiment where I took all of the starters I was keeping at the time and I tested them for how long it took them to double and then how long until they peaked (the highest level at which they fall back). I fed the starters and then measured the same amount into each jar and marked the level where the starter had risen each hour. It was fascinating because the starters had different capabilities or proofing times.

One starter was so fast at doubling that it only took three hours until it peaked and fell back. Well that might be good for a short, one day ferment for making a quick loaf of bread, but I wanted a starter that would keep on going hours after it was fed.

The average or standard starter has great leavening power for about six hours, starters with shorter capabilities should be used for quick breads and one day loafs. I have a starter that will peak in about ten hours and that is a great starter for the very long fermented doughs that I like to work with. An average sourdough starter will peak at around six hours at an average room temperature of around 72F/22C.

So test your starter and see what it can do. Also don't be surprised if your starter falls back once it peaks, but then rallies and rises up a small amount again. That can happen but the first time it falls back is its peak time. Once you know your starters peak time, you can adjust your bulk ferment to take advantage of your starter's capability. If your starter ferments too fast and you want to slow it down, add a pinch of salt. Salt slows down fermentation.

Float Test

A popular way to gauge whether your starter is ready to use in your formula after feeding it is to take some and see if it will float on top of water. Once it is bubbly and full of gasses it should float when it is ready. That is a very loose test though as a lower hydration starter would be heavier even when it is fully ready to use and a very high hydration starter won't hold the gasses and so may not pass the test even when it is ready. This test is mainly for a 100% hydration starter. The float test is not accurate, so don't rely on it.

Having Enough Starter for Your Formula

Let's say you've been feeding your starter 40 grams of flour and 40 grams of water each day. The evening before mixing dough, pour out all but 30 -50 grams of the starter and then feed it the amount the recipe or formula calls for. If the formula calls for 100 grams of starter, then add 50 grams of flour and 50 grams of water to your starter the night before you plan to use it.

Then after using the starter in your formula, continue to feed it on the former schedule or whatever you are comfortable with (if you want to keep more starter feed it more). If you need a lot of starter for a large batch of flapjacks or bread, pour out less of the starter then feed the sourdough starter lots more food and keep it in a warm or room temperature place.

Hint: You can find lots of free recipes/formulas and baking courses on my site at: **http://www.northwestsourdough.com.** Just look in the blog tab.

Starter Variations

Using Different Types of Flour

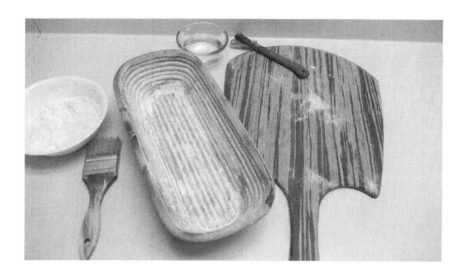

If you would like to have a whole wheat or a rye starter or any other different type of starter, continue to feed your starter every day, but feed it with your preferred flour instead of white flour. You may need to adjust the amount of water, because various types of flour are capable of absorbing different amounts of water. An established starter might slow down if you change its diet suddenly. Increasing the new flour while decreasing the old flour over a few days during feeding time can help with the transition.

You will need to feed your starter every day to keep it healthy. After two weeks, with daily feedings, your sourdough starter will be mature. Now you can have fun baking with your sourdough starter. You can refrigerate your new starter for short periods of time when it isn't being used, now that it is mature. Many bakers keep their sourdough starter in the refrigerator. When they want to bake, they will take out their starter, feed it and keep it at room temperature until it is active again, then use it to bake with, feed it again and store it in their refrigerator until they want to use it again.

NOTE: The above procedure is a simple way to begin your own starter. Some bakers use pineapple juice (or apple cider) instead of water, to feed their starter for the **first four days**. The acidity of the juice encourages the proper microorganisms to propagate. If you want to try using juice instead of water, you only need to use it for the first four days. After day four, feed your starter with flour and water. Don't use milk, sugar or any ingredients other than water and flour to feed your starter. *(see the Pineapple Juice Solution by Debra Wink)

Fresh whole grain flour has approximately 200 times the microorganisms* as white flour so using some whole grain flour really helps to get the starter fermenting. Rye flour or whole wheat flour are good choices to use in making your new starter.

Some bakers prefer to use all whole grain flour without any white flour. Whole grain flour absorbs more water than white flour, so expect a whole grain starter to be drier and add extra water if you feel it is too dry (use a different hydration level).

Your starter should have the consistency of thick pancake batter or a muffin batter when using white flour, a whole grain flour will be thicker. With time, the fermentation process weakens the gluten and the mixture is thinner and can have a layer of liquid on top (especially for higher hydration starters). That isn't a problem, just mix in the liquid, pour out half of your starter and continue to feed it.

When you are ready to use your mature starter, you will have to figure out how much you will need for your formula and adjust the amount that you feed your starter accordingly.

The warmer you keep your sourdough starter, the more often you will need to feed it. If you live in a warm area and need to slow down the fermentation of your starter then try adding a pinch of salt to slow your starter down, or adjust your ratio of starter to feed, pouring out more of the starter and giving it more food. You can also pour out most of the starter and feed it more often.

Whole grain starters often need to be fed more often or a higher ratio of food to starter to keep healthy since they ferment more quickly, you can also use a pinch of salt to help control over fermenting.

What Does Hydration Mean?

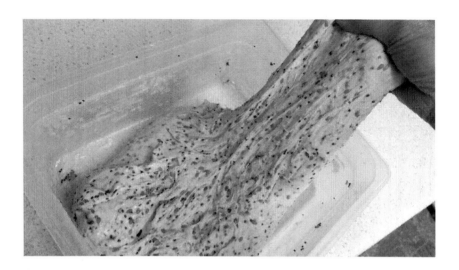

The term hydration as it applies to baking, means the percentage of water added to the dough, based on the weight of the flour. It basically means how wet a dough or batter is. The weight of the flour is always considered 100%. All of the other ingredient weights are based off of the weight of the flour. This is called Baker's Percentage.

If the weight of the water is 50% of weight of the flour, the dough is considered to be at 50% hydration. If your dough is 100% hydration, it means the water and flour in the dough are the same weight. For instance, dough made of 200 grams of water and 200 grams of flour would be a 100% hydration dough. Dough made with 100 grams of water and 200 grams of flour would be 50% hydration dough.

If I wanted to make 80% hydration dough, which is really wet by the way (Ciabatta dough), then I might add 800 grams of water to 1000 grams of flour and that would give me 80% hydration dough. Flour will absorb water differently, so it is not a fast and hard rule, but something to go by.

Taking Care of Your Starter

Once your starter is mature, at around two weeks, you can use it to make a variety of sourdough baked goods.

Feed your starter extra flour and water so you have enough for your dough. After using your starter, feed and store it, covered, at room temperature. If you keep your starter at room temperature, make sure to pour most of it out and feed it every day. Some bakers feed their starter two or three times a day. The minimum amount is once a day, a healthy amount is twice a day. If you refrigerate your starter, make sure to take it out once a week and feed it to keep it healthy. However, a starter can take a lot of neglect and still bounce back.

Cleaning the Container and Revitalizing a Bad Starter

If you neglect to discard and feed your starter on a regular basis, it can become sick. Bad bacteria can infect it or mold and slime can grow if it is unhealthy. Keeping the container clean and the sides scraped down are other ways to help your starter stay healthy. When there is a build-up of dried starter along the sides, try to scrape some of it out and discard the built up starter. Occasionally, take a small amount of your starter, like 30 grams, set it aside in a clean bowl. Then take the container and clean it out really well using only hot water. Don't use soap, detergent or bleach for cleaning the container.

When the container is clean, replace the reserved starter and feed it small quantities of food (50 grams of water and 50 grams of flour to start with). You can increase the amount of food as necessary depending upon your baking schedule.

Freezing your Starter

You can freeze your starter for a few months at a time. This is a great way to store the starter if you are going on vacation. The longer the starter is frozen, the less viable the microorganisms will be, so plan on using this storage method for a few weeks or months but not for a year. Frost free freezers can be hard on a starter because of the cycle of freezing and thawing. It is best to use a container to freeze the starter and place other items around it.

To freeze your starter, you need to make a low hydration dough ball. To make a low hydration dough ball, take some of your starter that has been fed previously and is vigorous. Add enough flour to make a piece of dense dough. Here is an example:

Mix together:
- 60 grams vigorous starter @100% hydration
- 30 grams flour

Mix and then knead the above ingredient together until you have a stiff dough ball. The dough ball will be around 50% hydration. Place it in a container or freezer bag, mark the date and freeze it. This makes a 90 grams size dough ball, if you would like a larger dough ball, double the formula above. To reuse it, thaw the dough ball, dissolve some of the dough into water and begin to feed it just like a regular starter. It might take a day or two but it should be bubbling soon.

Drying and Storing Your Starter

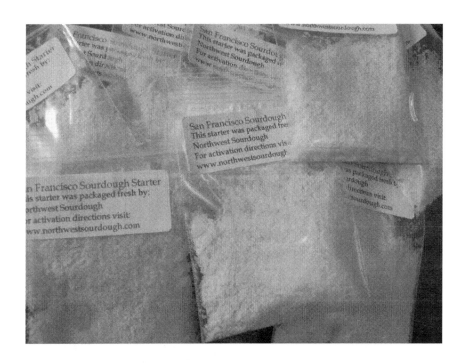

To keep a backup of your starter or to more easily send it to someone in the mail, dry it. I brought a starter back to life that was dried for over 50 years. It still worked!

To dry your starter, feed it the night before and make sure it is vigorous. Add extra water so it is thin like a thick paint. Then spread the starter out on a stretched piece of plastic wrap using a pastry brush. Allow it to dry completely, then crumble it and store it in an airtight container. No need to freeze dried starter, it lasts better at room temperature or someplace cool. Freezers with their defrost cycle aren't the greatest place for a dried starter.

A good way to store it is to use a mason jar with a screw band, a bail top jar or you can put it in a zip bag and place it in a plastic sealed container. A plastic bag might work, but it won't keep out bugs or rodents.

To reconstitute dried starter, add a tablespoon of the flakes to some warm water and begin feeding again like a regular starter. It can actually take as long to become stable again as a new starter, but you will start out with a known starter culture.

Suppliers of dried sourdough starters:

http://www.kingarthurflour.com

http://www.breadtopia.com

Slowing Down Fermentation

During the summer months ambient temperatures are warmer. Your starter and dough can over-ferment easily in hotter weather. Here are some ideas for slowing down your starter and dough if your surrounding temperatures are very warm:

To slow down the starter:

- Keep it cooler
- Feed less whole grains and instead use more white flour
- Add a pinch of salt
- Use ice water when feeding
- Try a lower inoculation (less starter to food ratio)

- Lower the hydration (you would only want to use the last one if you are storing it or using a low hydration motherdough)
- Use a tightly woven cloth over your starter (secure it with a rubber band) to allow it to breath and prevent heat buildup in a closed container*

In warmer weather you should reserve less of the starter when feeding and feed it more often.

To slow down your final dough:

- Do a shorter autolyse or skip the autolyse
- Use a pinch of salt when mixing the dough
- Try adding ice water when making your dough
- Keep your flour in cold storage
- Use formulas with a lower inoculation rate (use less starter in the dough)
- Keep the dough cool (try putting the whole container in the fridge more often)
- Chill the dough BEFORE shaping and retarding

- Use your starter when it's younger, after just a few hours of fermenting (not overly fermented and warm)
- Try using a cold motherdough or lievito madre for inoculation instead
- Put a pinch of sea salt in the motherdough or starter
- Use more white flour and less whole grains
- Mix and then chill the dough right away, letting it take a few days to ferment before using it

A sourdough starter culture is anaerobic and doesn't NEED oxygen to exist, although it likes oxygen just fine. The tightly woven cloth will just allow the heat to escape so it doesn't build up as much in a closed container. However, it may also evaporate more quickly.

TIPS

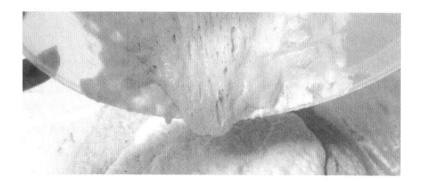

- Stir the starter well after feeding. Although it doesn't need air because it's anaerobic, it does like oxygen.
- Don't refrigerate your starter until it is mature at around two weeks (you may have to if you live where it's very warm).
- Clean the container with plain hot water when it needs cleaning.
- Don't use reactive metal when working with sourdough.
- A small pinch of salt can slow down fermentation in a starter.
- Don't feed your starter anything but flour and water.
- Test your starter and see what it can do.
- If you live where it's warm, pour out most of your starter before refeeding and feed more often.
- Keep your starter healthy by feeding and caring for it properly.

How to Make Motherdough @ 60% Hydration

A Different Kind of Starter (cold fermented starter)

Motherdough is pre-fermented dough from which other dough is made. The term "motherdough" may have a different meaning to different people. Motherdough in this book means dough that is kept cool while it is fermenting and then is used to flavor and/or leaven other dough to make delicious bread with complex flavor. When dough is kept cool during fermentation, the microorganisms have time to metabolize the sugars in the starch.

Cool fermentation also encourages acetic acid formation, together with bacterial and enzymatic activity, all of which enhance the flavor of the loaf.

To make motherdough you can use any hydration (add any amount of water) you wish, but usually a motherdough is a drier dough from 40 – 80% hydration, whereas a sponge or a poolish is closer to 100% hydration.

Many formulas/recipes utilize Motherdough. Motherdough is a cold pre-ferment which you make up and store in your refrigerator for some time. You can have a low hydration (like 60%) motherdough ferment in your refrigerator for a long time. You should leave it in your refrigerator for at least 3 – 4 days before using it. Motherdough needs time to ferment.

As long as the motherdough has some stretch to it and has not become runny, like glue, it can be used. Motherdough is sometimes used with another sourdough starter which is fresh and has plenty of wild yeast.

You can also feed your motherdough and keep it going in the fridge. I keep a 40% hydration motherdough in my fridge for months at a time. When kept for long periods of time, the motherdough pre-ferment is used for flavoring and adding acidity and protease enzymes to your freshly made dough, it wouldn't have enough power left to leaven new dough. When used for flavoring, I also use another fresh vigorous starter along with the motherdough in the formula to bring in the leavening power.

60% Motherdough Formula

In a 2 quart or 2 liter container which can be sealed, add together:

- **170 g - Vigorous fresh sourdough starter @ 100% hydration (fed within eight hours)**
- **170 g - Water**
- **340 g - Flour**

Mix all of the above ingredients and store, tightly covered, in your refrigerator for at least 3-4 days before using. This will make about 1.5 pounds/680 grams. Double this amount if you wish to keep some on hand for baking. Formulas for using your new starter and motherdough can be found on my site at Northwest Sourdough, in my book, "Discovering

Sourdough" and in my sourdough baking courses which you will find at http://www.northweststsourdough.com
There are many kinds of pre-ferments and sponges. Motherdough is only one type. There's a whole world of sourdough fun out there!

40% Motherdough Formula

A 40% motherdough is used in some of my baking courses. This VERY low hydration starter is used for flavoring and acidity not for leavening. It is usually kept fermenting for a very long time (months) in the refrigerator and is used whenever necessary. So here is a formula for making 40% motherdough.

You can find the full article on 40% motherdough here: http://www.northwestsourdough.com/?p=3077

40% motherdough using 100% hydration starter

- 6 oz/170g vigorous starter @ 100% hydration
- 5 oz/141g water
- 1 oz/28g whole wheat flour (freshly ground if you can get it)
- 16 oz/453g good strong bread flour

Total= 1 lb 12 oz/793g @ 40%

It takes some effort to incorporate such low hydration dough. So if you feel you can't knead in all the dough, walk away and let it set for 20 minutes and then come back and knead it some more. It will take a bit of time, but the dough will finally come together.

40% motherdough using 166% hydration starter:

- 157g of 166% starter (5.5 oz)
- 141g water (5 oz)
- 28g whole wheat flour (1 oz)
- 510g of bread flour (18 oz)

Total= 836 g (1 lb 13.5 oz) @ 40% hydration

Make this dough up and do what I said above, let it rot somewhere cool in a tightly covered container.

After a while, try a week or two, break apart a piece of the dough and if it looks crumbly or cottage cheesy, then it is ready, especially if it smells strongly sour. If you taste a piece of it, your tongue will curdle and you will make a "lemon" face. The outside of the seed dough will have a graying cast to it, don't worry, it won't hurt anything. I often scoop from the inside of the dough, but the outside works too.

50% Hydration Motherdough:

50% Starter sometimes called "Lievito Madre" is similar to a "Biga." A 50% starter is a low hydration starter that you ferment for a few days and then use as leavening and for flavor. It is a great leavening motherdough.

Add together:

- **100 grams of 100% starter (3.5 oz)**
- **175 grams water (6 oz)**
- **400 grams flour (14 oz)**

Mix together and let ferment (cold) for a few days before using. This formula will make:

675 grams of 50% motherdough (or around 1.5 pounds)

All of these starters and pre-ferments are used in numerous formulas and recipes which you can find online at: **http://www.northwestsourdough.com**

Continue Your Sourdough Journey

Now that you have a nicely fermenting sourdough starter, it's time to bake bread! When your starter is young, you can make pancakes, waffles, quick breads etc. Once it's strong enough (around two weeks old) then you can begin to bake bread.

For more information on how to bake the best bread in the world visit me at: **http://www.northwestsourdough.com**

About the Author

Teresa loves teaching serious home bakers, how to bake real sourdough bread! She worked at two different bakeries besides baking at home for over 40 years.

She published several books including a four volume book called, "Discovering Sourdough," "Extreme Fermentation" and also, "Make Your Own Sourdough Starter." Teresa also published her memoir titled: "Reach for Joy," under the pseudonym, TL Reys.
Her bread recipes and formulas from her books and blog have been featured on TV and spread all around the world through online forums, her active Facebook group, Perfect

Sourdough, her Youtube channel and her site, Northwest Sourdough.

She has been featured in numerous articles, magazines and interviews. She was selected as one of the top ten Udemy instructors in 2015 and now has ten sourdough baking courses on Udemy.

Most of all, Teresa loves to see YOU pull a crispy, crusty, holey sourdough loaf from your own oven! Yes, you can learn to bake the best bread in the world!

You can find Teresa's online sourdough baking courses by visiting here: **http://www.northwestsourdough.com**
The courses are online, at your own pace, accessible for your lifetime and you get a certificate upon completion! They feature by step learning with video and text lectures.

Resources

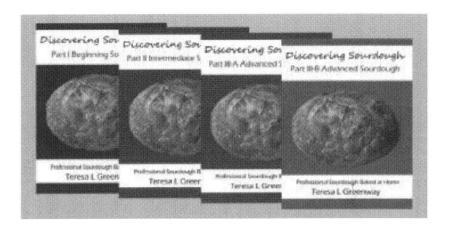

For more information see:
http://www.northwestsourdough.com

See over 250 videos on Northwest Sourdough's You Tube Channel at:
https://www.youtube.com/user/northwestsourdough
Find Teresa on Facebook in the group: Perfect Sourdough
Or on her blog at:
http://www.northwestsourdough.com/blog
For more baking fun try Teresa's four volume, 400 page book, "Discovering Sourdough," which you will find on Amazon and in her Etsy Shop, "Pixie Bakery."

Happy Baking Everyone!

Teresa

Made in the USA
Coppell, TX
05 January 2021

47581678R00030